Yes, You Can:

7 Keys to Student Success

MIKE NELSON

About Author

Mike Nelson grew up in West Philadelphia. In school, he was an average student at best, especially the years from middle school thru high school he had many academic challenges. To say he hated school would be an understatement because he absolutely, without a doubt, hated school-it was boring, plain and simple. He found very little interest doing anything related to academics. "My favorite 'subjects' where gym and lunch. Ha. Ha." (No seriously!)

Upon graduating, he took a chance by going to college as an academic risk student. His GPA was around 2.6 in high school, without studying or trying, and scored well below the average on his SAT'S. He almost got kicked out of college his GPA his first year was a 1.9. He was able to pull his GPA up and graduate. He knows what it's like to sit in a classroom, not understand anything being taught and struggle in silence.

"I know what it's like to be disengaged with tests and assignments. I have been the student who failed test after test. I have been that student doing just enough to get by, so not to fail, but desiring to do better academically; I just didn't know how."

Mike dug deep, wanted more for himself, so he learned, through several key adjustments in his thinking how to be a great student, to overcome academic challenges. He went from a 1.9 GPA and almost getting kicked out of college to almost 3.5 GPA, in a Master's Program.

Mike has been working diligently since 2011, not only with students of various ages, in many different capacities; but also as a student recruiter, motivational speaker, coach, admissions counselor, student advocate and educator. With all of his experiences, he is ready to show you how you can go from worst to first. Mike will show you how to go from average student to a great student, how to improve your GPA, and to never let academic challenges define your success as a student.

How did Mike Nelson go from academic risk student to successful Master's degree student? Put your seatbelt on and let's go for a ride, as we explore the 7 Keys to Student Success!

Table of Contents

Book Reviews

Thank you, thank you, thank you Mike Nelson! "Yes, You Can: 7 Keys to Student Success" is a must read for EVERY student and parent who is serious about ensuring a successful educational outcome. Mike delivers an easy read that is relevant and realistic and speaks directly to students. After several motivational presentations, I expected nothing less

- Dr. Toni Damon
Principal, Murrell Dobbins CTE High School

For any student looking to level up academically, get your hands on this book…now! In "Yes, You Can: 7 Keys to Student Success," Mike Nelson delivers honest and compelling words in an incredibly accessible way. Reading this book is like having your own personal inspirational and motivational coach in your back pocket. Don't miss this one!

- Cynthia Jones
Community Partnerships Coordinator
James G. Blaine Academics Plus

In "Yes, You Can: 7 Keys to Student Success," Mike Nelson lays out a plan for success for all students, high achieving and at-risk. Based on his own academic journey, Mike gives the reader a practical guide for achieving success. Through vivid testimonials and brief exercises readers are engaged in a multi-tiered process for decision making and setting attainable goals leading to academic success.

- Debora Borges-Carrera
Assistant Superintendent
School District of Philadelphia

"Yes, You Can: 7 Keys to Student Success," an innovative guide to learning, it is Mike Nelson's literacy breakout to the world! He delivers his message in a practical and understandable matter. He provides vivid and clear examples for each student to visualize their way to academic success. Each principle is designed to inspire and motivate students to be their best self. Through this guide students will have new tools to sharpen their skills such as being a critical thinker, problem solver and increase their learning motivation.

- Sonia Lewis
First Year Academic Coach
Pierce College

"Yes, You Can: 7 Keys to Student Success" is the right blend of motivation, personal connection and self-exploration for today's students. Any student looking to gain discipline, learn how to set goals and plan for their own success, will greatly benefit from putting the 7 keys to success to work. For students who doubt themselves, through the help of this book you can put yourself on the path to mastering your academic life. Now is the time to tell yourself, "Yes, You Can!" If not now, then when?

- Jason Smith
Director of College Support
KIPP Philadelphia Schools

Dedication

This book is dedicated to the three women in my life who have my heart. To my dear mother, who has always been a constant supporter of all of my endeavors. You have helped shape me into the man I am today. Thank you for sacrificing so much for me, in order that I might be where I am presently. I love you more than you'll ever know.

To my Grandmother, for the wisdom you've always given me, and the reminders of always making sure that I will never forget where I come from. Thank-you for reminding me to always remain humble; sharing the impact that I could have on people's lives if I would dare to follow after God.

Last, but not least, to my beautiful wife Adrian, who has been there through everything, including all of my crazy ideas and played a big part in my transformation from boyhood to manhood. There are no words that I could express for you to understand my gratitude.

Who should read the 7 Keys to Student Success?

➤ If you are a student who has academic challenges-this book is for you.

➤ If you are a student who has struggled with confidence in your own abilities-this book is for you.

➤ Do you have a desire to want to do better academically, but you are unsure what steps need to be taken? This book is for you.

➤ Are you an average student looking to become a good student? Are you a good student looking to become a great student? This book is for you.

➤ Are you looking to improve your GPA? This book is for you.

➤ Get to another level academically? This book is for you.

Getting The Most Out of This Book

This book is designed to act as a workbook to achieve greater academic success. Use this book to record your goals, achievements and ideas in becoming a better student.

Upon completion of the book, the goal is to continually apply the 7 steps learned in the book to achieve greater success.

Here are suggestions on how to get the most results from this book:

➤ This book follows a logical sequence, however, each chapter can be read as a stand-alone chapter.

➤ If you want to get more assistance with achieving your greatest academic success, please reach out to Mike at www.MikeNelsonspeaks.com.

➤ Complete each exercise as you come upon them in each chapter.

➤ Read the book numerous times-finding value each time.

➤ The ACTION is critical; nothing happens until you become proactive and take action. I promise, taking action will produce results and break through academic growth.

Introduction

The 7 Keys to Student Success is for students to start believing "they can" achieve their academic greatness-they can be the student they have always desired to become.

What is the book all about?

This book focuses on those aspects of student success that both directly or indirectly increase personal achievement.

How is the book organized?

The book has 7 chapters. Each chapter has been organized in a manner that the student, you, will be able to see a practical example, a background story on what I have learned and gone through and then an exercise in which you, the student, can do. The exercises are meant for you to pause, think about the answer, then write it down in the space provided. The book is not only your guide and resource in achieving academic success, but it is also a journal to scribble, jot down and look back at the answers you have written throughout the book.

Why is the book unique?

The book focuses purely on how to achieve academic success. Unique features include:

➤ Critical Thinking Skills

➢ Student Empowerment

➢ Study Motivation

➢ Problem Solving Skills

Any single idea, action, quote or fact mentioned in the book has a potential to transform you and your life.

As someone once said, "***Nothing happens until someone does something.***" Over the years, I have interacted with hundreds of students, all looking to increase their academic success. Without the knowledge, skill, attitude or the proper tools, their journey is a tough one. I wrote this book because I feel I can guarantee that the concepts, suggested exercises, and actions I present in the book, can make a huge difference to their academic success.

"GREATER
ACADEMIC
ACHIEVEMENT
LEADS
TO GREATER
PERSONAL
FREEDOM"
-MIKE NELSON

In the grand scheme of things, achieving our greatest academic potential can help with every students' biggest challenges such as:

➤ Study Habits

➤ Self Confidence

➤ Dropout Rate

This book is the result of more than 1,000 hours of personal and hands on experience with students and finding a solution to assisting students to do better academically. It contains many of the best ideas and strategies I have learned, taught, discovered and implemented over many years.

I have tried to keep the language and layout of the book as simple as possible. E. F. Schumacher once stated, "Any intelligent fool can make things bigger and more complex...It takes a touch of genius-and-a lot of courage to move in the opposite direction."

A final note.

Any knowledge seeker needs to pass through a four-step process:

1. Access knowledge by reading, listening or watching
2. Understand it
3. Accept it
4. Implement it

"THERE ARE

NO

BENEFITS

TO KNOWLEDGE

UNTIL

YOU

IMPLEMENT

IT"

{ -MIKE NELSON }

Chapter 1: Decision Making

"THE DECISIONS WE MAKE,
ARE JUST AS
IMPORTANT AS
THE DECISIONS
WE DON'T MAKE"

{ -MIKE NELSON }

The date was July 8, 2010. Ohio native, LeBron James sent shock waves through the entire sports world, when he decided that he would no longer play for the Cleveland Cavaliers as he was joining the Miami Heat. LeBron's departure would be known as "The Decision." He was the former #1 overall pick in 2003. He spent his first seven years in the NBA playing for the Cleveland Cavaliers, winning multiple MVP awards, and even taking the Cavaliers to the NBA Finals in 2007; a place the franchise had never been before. How was it possible for hometown superstar LeBron James, to make such a depart from his hometown state of Ohio?

LeBron did what we, as students, have to do at some point in our academic career. **HE MADE A DECISION ABOUT HIS FUTURE!** (Read That Again). Think about it, when was the last time you asked yourself, "What kind of student do I want to be?" Making a decision about the student you want to become, is the first key to your student success. Notice, I am not too concerned just yet, if you struggle in any areas academically. The reason being is because it doesn't matter if you don't make a decision about the kind of student you would like to become!

"EVERYONE WON'T

APPROVE OF

YOUR DECISIONS

{ AS A STUDENT" }

-MIKE NELSON

When LeBron James decided to leave Cleveland and go to Miami, the Cleveland fans were so upset, they burned their LeBron jersey's-criticism ensued not only from fans but sports commentators and sports writers. When you say to yourself, "I have to do better academically" and you make the choice to do so, there might be friends who will "burn your jersey." They might look at you differently; upset that your decision doesn't involve some of the old behaviors that you use to do. There is an old saying, "Sometimes in life, to do something great, you have to leave others behind." I am telling you, leave anyone behind that will not support you in your decision to become better personally and academically. I know for some of you this may be tough, because your friends are very important, but that certificate, diploma or degree is even more important.

To this date, LeBron James has never once apologized for leaving Cleveland to play for the Miami Heat. Neither should you! Don't you ever apologize for wanting to do better! Don't you dare apologize for making a commitment to becoming a better student! Your decision is not personal you just have to decide to do what's best for you and your future. LeBron James looked around at his team and realized the people he was around were hindering him from the ultimate prize; the NBA Championship. For you as a student, your NBA championship is that certificate, diploma or degree. Kobe Bryant, had a great quote when asked about friends, he said, "Friends hang sometimes, but banners hang forever!" I want you to replace the word "banners," for whatever certificate, diploma or degree you will be hanging on your wall. Remember that word the next time your friends, family members or people you meet try telling you to do something that will not help you to become a better you or a better student.

Jim Rohn, motivational speaker said, "You are the total sum of the 5 people you surround yourself with." This means, if you truly want to gauge how successful you will be, look at those who are within your circle of friends. In my junior year of high school, I had to make the decision about my friends, because they would influence my future academics and the goals I had set for myself.

(Exercise)

Below you see two columns. On the left I want you to locate the word **FRIENDS**. List every single person that you consider a friend. For some of you this might be hard because you have a lot of people you are connected with, but I want you to think of 5. For those of us who aren't connected to many people, write as many people as you can think of who you would consider friends.

After you are finished, in the column to the right labeled **HELPERS**, I want you to list those from the list **FRIENDS** column who can help you personally and academically. I don't care if it's only 1-3 people, no matter how old or young they are, these are the individuals you need to surround yourself with.

WHY? Because friends don't let each other fail! If a name from the friend's side made it to the column labeled helpers, then most likely neither want to fail.

FRIENDS	HELPERS

Don't feel guilty if you have to stop hanging around some "friends." Chances are, if you don't stop **HANGING** around them you won't ever be able to **HANG** that diploma or degree on your wall one day. (Reread that again!). This doesn't make those individuals bad people, it just means where you are trying to go academically and personally, not EVERYONE can ride with you! There is no time to be wasted, share with your friends (CALL, TEXT, or in person) tell them how excited you are to have them as friends; tell them what you are trying to get done in terms of your academics, and how you'd be honored if they could assist you. I would say 99% of those you tell, unless they aren't genuine friends, will be glad to assist you!

"CHANCES ARE, IF YOU DON'T HANG WITH THE RIGHT PEOPLE, YOU'LL NEVER BE ABLE TO HANG THAT DIPLOMA OR DEGREE ON YOUR WALL"

-MIKE NELSON

For some of you, I get it, you're gifted as a student. My sister Candace was; school always came so easy for her; barely studying. Sometimes the work was so easy that she would become bored. So for all of my students who don't struggle academically, this portion is for you.

Your greatest challenge may not ever come in the classroom; your greatest challenge will be in the DECISIONS you make as a student. Please, don't be fooled into thinking because you may be gifted academically, or school isn't a struggle, that your decision making doesn't matter. There were individuals when I was in college, who didn't struggle academically, but ended up not graduating. Why? Because they made poor choices along the way that stopped them from completing what they had started. Just because you're a good student, doesn't mean you can't improve to become a GREAT student-a great student can improve to be a PHENOMENAL student-if you're phenomenal, help another student get to the level you are on! There is always room to grow personally and academically-there has been and always will be something that you can improve on.

Let me explain why A's don't randomly happen, or for that matter, no grades randomly happen. Every single grade that you will not get, but EARN as a student, will be because you made a good decision or a bad decision. I remember in college, I had a professor who started everyone off with the letter grade of an F. Most classes, everyone starts off with the letter grade of an A. My professor's thinking was he would not give a grade, but that every student would decide what grade that they wanted to have. We had to do a certain amount of work to receive different grades. So when you passed the letter F work, you would move on to the letter D work, pass that and move on to the letter C work, and so forth. Each level you passed, as you can imagine, the assignments got harder. Everyone in the class made the choice of what grade they desired and no one could say, "Well the professor gave me a bad grade." Nope, we all MADE A DECISION about the grade we would earn. I need you today, to decide what kind of grades you will earn, and what kind of student will you decide to become.

(Exercise)

Accountability Decision

Write these statements on a sticky note or use a dry erase marker on a mirror. Recite these daily. Give them to the people you listed as HELPERS in the previous exercise; have them help you remain accountable.

I chose to get _____ (**insert grade**).

I chose to be a _____ student.

Through all my years of education, currently pursuing a Master's degree, I cannot think of a time where I was given a grade; every single grade I received was from what I earned, because of the decision I made. Think about it, even when you are not choosing to study, not choosing to turn in your assignments, you are still making a choice. I always tell students; the decisions you make are just as important as the decisions you don't make. LeBron James knew he was one of the top basketball players while in Cleveland. He could have willingly decided to not do anything, and probably would have still been one of the top talents in basketball (Instead he chose to make a decision to be uncomfortable and leave his comfort zone in Cleveland). Are you willing to make the necessary decisions to leave your comfort zone? I don't know what your comfort zone is, but be willing and open to get out of it, as a student. I MADE A DECISION.

After all the years of academic struggles, I realized that I was good at staying in my comfort zone, and hiding, until I got to college and realized that I could not hide anymore. As a student, please save yourself the time and the energy, make a DECISION that no matter what happens, no matter how difficult it gets, you will give it your very best. Every day when you get up, I want you to say, "I will give today my very best, because I deserve the best."

"THE DECISION TO QUIT
IS OFTEN EASIER,
**THAN THE DECISION
TO KEEP GOING"**
-MIKE NELSON

Does your life as a student get difficult, it sure does! For those who may be reading this in high school, as puberty takes on a life of its own, and trying to balance school work, it can be challenging. For those who are in college, the pull between social life, parties, academics and a taste of the real world can be challenging as well. For my graduate students, maybe marriage, working, and family, while balancing school work is definitely challenging. I'll be honest, I had no idea if I had what it took to graduate college; my first semester GPA, 1.9 was a sure sign telling me I did not. I remember asking myself repeatedly if I had what it takes to accomplish what I set out to do-the first person in my immediate family to graduate college. There were times where I would be up for hours debating on leaving; I thought college was more difficult than what I originally expected. It wasn't until I had a tough conversation with myself, and thought about the alternative to quitting. My choices were limited. On one hand, go back to West Philly and live with my parents. However, personally, I didn't want to be known as "the guy" who quit. There were plenty of those people that I knew, and I was determined not to be one of them. On the other hand, **I HAD MADE A DECISION**. I said to myself, that no matter what happens, **I WILL NOT QUIT AND I WILL GRADUATE**!

For you, those words need to be repeated to yourself every day; especially if you struggle academically like I did. So there it is, my decision was made no matter what happened, **I MUST GRADUATE**. Then, I got a phone call that dropped me to my knees-my sister had been hit by a drunk driver, and was in critical condition at the hospital. As I was processing all that had happened my new decision to graduate, and my sister who was in critical condition, what was I to do? As I arrived and saw her twice the size of her normal body, I thought my academics can be put on hold. As I was home, I looked in the mirror and told myself **"YOU MADE A DECISION STICK TO IT."**

Just because you are a student, life will continue to happen, and you don't get exempt from the tribulations of life because you are in school. So now what you have to do, is find a way to get through whatever obstacle that may be holding you back. I promise you, I didn't know how, but I knew I had to get across the finish line, I knew for me this was **MY DECISION**, it was now or never. You may be in a course that seems challenging, you maybe be starting High school and thinking how will I adjust? You may be in High school and feel like school is a waste of time, you may be in College thinking I'm not smart enough to get that degree. **YES, YOU ARE**. You are smart enough to pass that course, what helped me every time something got challenging, I just remembered **I MADE A DECISION**, you see when you make a decision, it doesn't matter what happens because you have already chosen the outcome.

You've already decided you will pass that test, you've already decided I will pass that course, you decided I will get that certificate, degree or diploma. My sister ended up living, and I am so happy I decided to not quit because life got difficult. However, there will be more challenges up the road, but once you are able to get through one, it gets a little bit easier.

My junior year I had an uncle pass away from Aids, few months later another uncle died of prostate cancer. Although, I was hurt, I thought to myself my decision was made 2 years ago to graduate. That is why again, I am not concerned if you're challenged academically you can always work on that, but if you haven't made a decision to pass that course, if you haven't made a decision to pass that test, if you haven't made a decision to get that certificate, diploma or that degree it will be easy to quit. The decision for you to **KEEP GOING** has to be stronger than the decisions to **QUIT**!

(Exercise)

Write down 7 reasons of why making the decision not to quit is important, after you write down your reasons, take a picture of it with your cell phone and save it. Every time you feel like quitting, remember why YOU Can't QUIT, because of the decisions you have listed.

1. _____

2. _____

3. _____

4. _____

5. _____

6. _____

7. _____

Nobody graduates by accident-fact. At the minimum level, if someone has graduated then it means somewhere along the way, **A DECISION** was made. If someone decides to fail a class, drop a course, or not graduate, **A DECISION** was made. Once I realized no professor, teacher, or my academic challenges could control what I could do, or who I could become, the course for the rest of my life changed forever! I am not saying that I don't have courses that aren't challenging, or the circumstances of life don't happen to me. But what I am telling you is, that you have to **MASTER THE ART OF NOT GIVING UP**. This goes back to my original stance; which I hope you are beginning to see "**MY DECISION**."

Here's something to think about. Why leave your academic future up to a professor or teacher to decide if you will pass? For some, you may feel as if your teacher or professor doesn't like you; if that is the case, don't leave your grade up to them. If you take care of business in the classroom, your professor or teacher has no choice but to give you the grade that you've **EARNED**. It goes back to you! You, as a student, are responsible for every choice that you make in and out of the classroom. You have to start making decisions. Is that game on my cellphone putting me anywhere closer to graduating and my goals? Spending too much time on social media, is that pushing you towards graduation? NO! NO AND NO AGAIN. Where you spend most of your time tells you where your decision making is.

"YOU AS A STUDENT ARE

RESPONSIBLE

{ FOR EVERY }

CHOICE THAT

YOU MAKE IN

AND OUT OF THE

≡ CLASSROOM" ≡

-MIKE NELSON

Graduating from college was quite the experience for me-as I walked across the stage and heard I was a college graduate, I shed tears, because I realized from that moment on, anything was possible for me. Important to note-I am not an emotional person. During my walk across the stage though, I realized a small decision I made 4 years prior led to that moment. The decisions we make can inspire others; there were plenty of times that I wanted to give up and quit. I just couldn't stomach telling my mother, who never attended college, that it was too hard; or telling my little brother he should start something that I myself couldn't finish.

I say all that to say this: You'll never know what you can accomplish academically, if you quit. Come on! I'm a kid from West Philly who graduated college, who continues my academic studies at the Graduate level. I don't say that to brag, I say that to let you know what's possible if you make the right decisions. I was determined to never let "life chose for me" but to stand up and let it be known, my academics will be dictated around the **CHOICES THAT I MAKE**. What my family and friends never understood was all the times I wanted to give up, and the times I thought about quitting; **MY DECISION** is what allowed me to walk across the stage at graduation. Just as LeBron James made a choice to become a champion and put himself in a position, that one day his decision, would become a reality. Why can't you? Yes, you deserve to earn the best grades possible. You deserve to walk across a stage. You deserve to become a better student. So I ask you this question: What are you waiting for? **MAKE A DECISION**!

If you are like me, you need to see it to believe it! So what I did was start small, writing down things that would happen if I didn't make smart choices academically. I also wrote down things that could happen if I made smart choices academically. Again, this is so simplistic. I call this the **RESULT EFFECT**, because things in life have results based on the decisions we make!

See the two examples below of the **RESULT EFFECT**.

1. If I don't go to class, I'll miss out on information. If I miss out on the information, I might fail the test. If I fail the test, I might get a bad grade. If I get a bad grade, I might fail the course. I fail the course, the **RESULT EFFECT** is, I might not graduate.

2. If I go to class, I should get the right information. I get the information; I can study for the test. I study for the test; I can pass the test. If I repeat these steps, I can pass the rest of my classes, The **RESULT EFFECT** is, I graduate!

Did you see that in both scenarios decisions had to be made, and both had different results because of those choices.

(Exercise)

Write down 7 academic decisions in the far left column. In the middle column, write down either I CAN or I CAN'T MAKE. In the far right column, write what the result effect will be from the choices.

ACADEMIC DECISION	I CAN / I CAN'T MAKE	RESULT EFFECT
Go to class	I can make	Graduate

Chapter 2: Accountability

"STUDENT
ACCOUNTABILITY
MEANS
YOU ARE RESPONSIBLE
FOR WHAT HAPPENS IN
YOUR ACADEMICS
{ AND YOUR LIFE" }
–MIKE NELSON

I find it interesting, with the hundreds of students I have had conversations with and have helped throughout the years, there has always been one missing piece hindering students from truly achieving student success. The missing piece is accountability.

What exactly is student accountability? I like to say it is simply taking responsibility for what has or hasn't happened in your academics. Before every motivational presentation, I always speak with students, and ask the question, "How are you doing in school?" The majority of students say they are doing well, while there are some who are very open, and admit some of the challenges and struggles they face. I always hear what I like to call, "Blame On." This term simply means that whatever the student is struggling with, he or she has to find someone or something to blame it on.

As you can imagine, I've heard everything from "my dog ate my homework" (when not turning in assignments), my teacher or professor doesn't like me, school is boring, the work is too hard, and my personal favorite, "I don't like school." While some of the above statements might be true, and I say this because I sincerely care about you, **NOBODY CARES**!

Remember the rule of thumb, "Accountability = Responsibility." You are responsible for your grades, **YOU**! When you as a student, are not holding yourself accountable when it comes to your grades and learning, it is easy to get side tracked with the many different distractions that surround each of us daily. I found this to be extremely true my first year in college.

(Exercise)

We all tend to put the blame on someone or something when things don't go our way, instead of asking the question, "What do I need to do differently?"

The rule of thumb is: if you can single handedly control the outcome of something, then that means, you are responsible.

List 7 things you can do better academically in the first column. The second column, write one way you plan on making that happen.

I can do better academically	I plan on making better
Raise my grade in Science by 1 letter grade.	*Study an extra 30 minutes each night*

"SOMETIMES

WE OFTEN

LEARN

ACCOUNTABILITY

AFTER THE DAMAGE

HAS BEEN DONE"

-MIKE NELSON

It was my second semester of my freshman year of college; barely made it through my first semester, and thought to myself, "How will I be able to get through the next?" Somehow, someway I found myself staring at my syllabus in disappointment, feeling as if I would never be able to get the work done. In one of my classes I had a professor who was very strict, the first day of class he told us, "Whatever you do, you cannot afford to miss a test". He said it so many times, I had begun to get annoyed, so I asked my roommate at the time, "Why does he keep saying that?" Neither of us knew, so I just dismissed it as a "professor being a professor." I knew we had our first examine of the class coming up, and as the exam was approaching, I kept saying to myself, "I'll study eventually" and eventually never came. Looking back, I am shocked as to how much accountability I lacked, not only in that particular experience but my entire undergraduate experience. I had the nerve to actually think I could pass a test in a subject, without studying, I wasn't even strong in.

The night before the exam, I spent time at the gym playing basketball with friends; knowing this test was something I wasn't prepared for. To make matters worse, I decided to stay up all night, and I didn't even think to crack open a textbook. I thought to myself, "I got this." Finally, in the very early hours, I fell asleep-class started at 8:30 a.m. When I opened my eyes a few hours later, it was about 12 noon;

my roommate and I had both overslept. I thought it was no big deal. I knew I would barely get through the class with a D grade, and if I studied for the final, which was worth a big percentage of the final grade, I would hold my D grade and pass the class.

The final was fast approaching and I had a gut feeling I wasn't going to pass the test; I had other finals to study for, and this particular subject was not my strongest. I ended up taking the final because my grade was already borderline passing, my final grade stood as an F because I didn't do well on the final. This should not surprise anyone reading this-I didn't study and I made the decision to not study, therefor I did not do well-I failed. A few days after the final, I had emailed my professor to see if I could talk with him, and like most professors he said yes. I set the meeting up for the following day so I would have time to figure out what I would say to him.

As I was walking over to his office, I thought, "Well, I will just tell him that I missed the first test because I had overslept; he should understand." When I had arrived at his office and sat down, I thought to myself, "I got this." I had schemed a plan to get myself at least a passing grade so I wouldn't have to repeat the course. As we began to talk, I was 100% positive that I would either be given a chance to take the first test again or he would curve my grade so I could pass. Again, I said to myself "I got this." However, the conversation took a completely different turn. My professor simply asked, "Why hadn't I come to him earlier after missing the first test?"

Usually I am a quick thinker, but I found myself not being able to answer. I simply said, "Because."

He looked at me with raised eyebrows and said, "Well Mr. Nelson, it's funny you didn't come to me when you thought it wasn't affecting your grade, but now you see that you will not pass the course, and you decide now is the time to do something, about a test you missed months ago?"

I looked down at the ground and was embarrassed. He looked at me with conviction and said, "Son I'll see you next year."

For one of the first times in my life I couldn't get myself out of a situation. For some of you reading this, because you have a charismatic personality or "higher" intelligence you are able to get yourself out of situations, but I am here to tell you, that your day will come when your charm, charisma or intelligence won't work in your favor. To make matters worse, when I arrived back to my dorm room, and asked my roommate how he did on the final exam, he told me he passed. I asked him if missing the first test had affected his final grade. He said, "no." I stood there and wondered if the professor gave him a passing score because he did well on the final exam, or allowed him to take the test over. He told me he went to go talk to him, after he overslept. I was upset that he didn't tell me he went to go talk to the professor about his grade, and secondly, in my mind, the professor I believed **GAVE** me a failing grade, rather than realizing that is the grade, I **EARNED**. I went from thinking, "I got this, to no I don't have this."

-MIKE NELSON

I started to play "Blame On," whatever or whoever I could find to blame for why I didn't pass that course. Think about that, I **BLAMED OTHERS FOR WHAT I FAILED TO DO**. That in of itself doesn't make sense. How could I blame someone for something I committed to do and didn't do it! Far too many students play the "Blame On" game. If we as students don't perform where we think we should be, we are quick to put the responsibility on someone or something else. Let me say this, you'll never reach your full potential academically or personally by playing "Blame On."

I appreciate all the professors, teachers and tutors who go about their business of doing everything in their power to support students. However, don't let yourself become confused as the ultimate responsibility falls on you.

Here I was a 19-year-old making excuses for why I didn't pass a class. I wish you guys could have heard me; I was reaching for excuses. I tried to convince myself that the excuses that I was telling myself actually made sense. I said to myself, "My professor didn't want me to pass nor did he help me." That statement was far from the truth as I had never emailed him until I knew I had failed. Not once did I reach out and ask for any type of help.

Looking back, I know I made the wrong decision. The decision I made, "I got this." Please students, do me a favor-don't suffer in silence. If you know that you are struggling, please say something to your teacher or professor. That is a part of being accountable; making sure you have someone who will help you through the process, and will not allow you to make an excuse.

"THIS IS MY LIFE,

THIS IS MY EDUCATION,

I WILL SUCCEED OR FAIL,

BECAUSE OF ME "

-MIKE NELSON

As of today's date, I give you permission to never make another excuse. For some of us, the reason we cannot move forward in our life and our academics suffer, is because of the excuses we make. Stop letting your excuses hold you back from what you can do, and what kind of student you can become. I blamed my roommate for why I had to repeat the class I failed, when it was never his fault in the first place. It wasn't his responsibility to make sure I passed my classes.

No other student or friend is solely responsible for your academics, you are! I blamed me failing the class on the fact that I came from West Philly, and my high school didn't prepare me for college. I began to realize I failed that course because I willingly chose to. I failed that class because I had not taken responsibility and ownership of doing what I was supposed to be doing. I said I wanted to go to college. I said I wanted to succeed academically. I thought it was everyone else's job to make sure I passed my courses by turning in work assignments and taking my tests. Say this with me, "This is my life, this is my education and I will succeed or fail because of me."

(Exercise)

Here is what I need you to do. I need you to make a list of at least 7 bad things academically that have happened to you (failed test, academic probation, repeated grade level, bad grade on an assignment, etc.) In the middle column, place who was to blame. The last column (SOLUTION) put a way you plan to NEVER allow that bad thing to happen again.

In most instances, **WE** should blame ourselves! As I made a list of all the failed tests, bad grades, etc., I realized **I WAS** 100% responsible for all that had happened to me academically.

BAD THINGS	WHO IS TO BLAME	SOLUTION
Failed Test	*Me*	*Ask for help. Study more.*

"SUCCESSFUL STUDENTS HOLD EACH OTHER ACCOUNTABLE"

-MIKE NELSON

I need you to find friends that are willing to hold you accountable. I need you to have friends who aren't afraid to tell you straight up and be honest of the things you might be doing wrong. I'll never forget the power of this principle. My accountability partner was my roommate; he understood that I had academic challenges, so we would meet once a week to review how I was doing in my classes. I needed an accountability partner, as do many of you.

The problem I have identified with many students, is that they would rather not listen to anyone but themselves, however, **YOU** only can take **YOU** so far. When you have an accountability partner, something strange happens; it's this feeling of, "I don't want to let them down." Your accountability partner will be able to help guide you, and keep you in check. Please whatever you do, don't be like me, and think, "I got this," because it didn't take long for me to realize, "I don't have this."

When choosing your accountability partner, be sure that he or she is someone you can trust, and someone who is a great student. Two students with academic struggles, attempting to help each other academically, might not be the best solution. Your accountability partner is there to **HELP**, not do any work for you. That is your job as a student; to complete your work.

Accountable students turn in classwork assignments on time; accountable students make sure that they are well prepared to take exams. Accountable students don't make excuses for why they aren't seeing the results they desire to see. Spending time making excuses of why you may have not passed a test, or turned in an assignment, distracts you from the time you could be doing other things to ensure you become a successful student. Being accountable as a student, you can look yourself in the mirror and know that you have given your very best.

(Exercise)

1. Find an accountability partner. Write their name. _____. Tell them you would like to meet weekly to talk about any struggles or challenges you might be facing.

2. What areas in your life do you lack responsibility in? Write in your top 3.

   a. _____

   b. _____

   c. _____

3. Do you play "Blame On?" Meaning, you have to blame someone or something for your academic failures. [See BLAME ON exercise on page 29]

   How many days can you go without making an excuse?

   _____.

4. How do you see yourself changing by being more accountable for your academics?

   a. _____

   b. _____

   c. _____

5. In general, are you a responsible person? How does this relate to your academics?

_____

_____

_____

_____

_____

_____

Do you have anyone who can vouch for you, that you are responsible? This can be anyone and you do not have to write their name down.

Chapter 3: S.W.A.G.

(Students with Academic Goals)

"STUDENTS WHO SET

GOALS POSITION

THEMSELVES

FOR SUCCESS"

-MIKE NELSON

Goal setting is vital to your success as a student, I cannot emphasize this point enough. Does school seem boring to you or do you find yourself daydreaming in class? If yes, that is the same answer I would have responded with years ago and it wasn't until I understood the power of goal setting, that my academics began to shift.

Growing up, school was always a challenge for me; what was being taught never interested me. This is no disrespect to any of the teachers or professors, but I just found myself not to be too concerned with what was being taught. Again, the best part for me about school, was lunch and gym class, (laughs) seriously it was. In high school at lunch, I was free to talk with my friends, and in college, I was free at either lunch or dinner to do the same. I remember the days of school being so boring that I would catch myself falling asleep. The only reason I would wake up, was when my head would begin to drift so low that I would almost fall out of my chair, hitting the corner of the desk. OUCH! So, how did I manage to no longer be bored with school?

It all started by me setting academic goals. The goals I set, forever changed the way I approached my academics. This is for my students who are bored with school. **SET ACADEMIC GOALS!** I promise you it works. It will give you a sense of meaning and purpose. It gives you a reason to show up to school every day, and give nothing less than your very best. Setting academic goals has absolutely nothing to do if in fact you like the subjects that are actually being taught. The subject being taught no longer matters; it is about the academic goals that you set for yourself.

Please, don't get fooled into thinking that you have to love every single subject, because you don't and most likely, won't. However, you at least need to learn about the subject, and become proficient in the subject; oh and by the way, pass the subject. For some of my classes, I knew most likely I would never use that information again. Even though the subject was boring, I knew I had certain academic goals that required I at least do my very best, or it could potentially stop me from reaching my academic goals. I wish I would have discovered academic goal setting years prior, saving me from boredom and the occasional bump and bruise on my head from falling asleep. Once I discovered the trick of setting goals, I was no longer bored in classes. Why? Because I was too focused on my academic goals of getting a certain grade, that I chose to do whatever it took to make sure that my academic goals would be reached. Again, after I made the decision that I would no longer accept being an average student, I came up with a game plan on how I was going to make sure these goals would happen. Remember back to our LeBron James story of him deciding to go to Miami. He had professional goals in mind when he began with the Cavaliers; he got tired of losing. So, he did whatever it took to reach his professional goals. He moved to Miami. Much like LeBron, as a student **YOU** have to **DECIDE** to do whatever it takes to reach your goals.

"ACADEMIC GOALS
HAVE NOTHING TO
DO WITH IF YOU
LIKE THE SUBJECT,
IT'S ABOUT
CHALLENGING
YOURSELF"

{ -MIKE NELSON }

(Exercise)

Again, because I believe you have to see it to believe it, write down 7 academic goals you would like to achieve in the first column. Your goals can be for the school year, this semester or even this month or week. After writing down each goal, write in the second column marked EFFECT ON GRADES, what type of effect the academic goal will have on your grades.

Academic Goals	Effect on Grades
Use flash cards to memorize stuff taught in class	*Will receive an A instead of a B*

Were you able see how the things you said you wanted to achieve academically is a direct result of setting goals. Your academics would be that much better as a result.

My question to you is, "**WHY HAVEN'T YOU STARTED?**"

It was the end of my sophomore year in college, and I remember saying to myself that something had to change going into my junior year. Once I received all of my classes, and the syllabus', I thoroughly looked over every single assignment, and began to think about those assignments. Because I had set academic goals, I was preparing myself for the work I had to do.

Students who set goals, understand that they are going to have to study, turn in assignments, and complete homework to get those academic goals accomplished. When I was in high school, goal setting was something I probably would have laughed at. Only reason being, is because I had yet to understand the power of what setting academic goals could do. Again, being honest with myself I did not say I wanted a 4.0, while desiring to have a 4.0 is great, I understood I had too many responsibilities to have a 4.0. So, what I did was, I told myself that "this semester I will have a 3.0."

For some of you reading this who feel as if a 3.0 it too low to shoot for, by all means please shoot for something higher. Maybe a 4.0 is a goal you feel would be achievable; I am fine with your choice. You, and only you, need to feel comfortable about setting your academic goals. Now, for those of you who may shoot for the extreme opposite-I am going to shoot for the letter grade of D, let me stop you right in your tracks. You are smarter than that, and you deserve more than that. You can get a letter grade of a D, by not evening trying. If you are setting academic goals with your friends, don't let what they set for themselves discourage you. Set an academic goal that will be challenging but also will be doable. If you have never received a 4.0 it will be difficult, but not impossible to achieve. School and sometimes learning present challenges that can frustrate us as students and what we don't need, is any added, unnecessary pressure. You are more likely to achieve something in life by making it a goal, than to thinking it will just happen.

As a student, you need to commit yourself to academic excellence! There are no excuses of why any student should be in class, and not have any idea of what kind of grades they would like. We as students should know exactly what kind of GPA we want, and how we would like to start and finish every school year or semester.

"BECOME
MARRIED TO
YOUR
ACADEMIC
GOALS"
-MIKE NELSON

If I could change one thing about my academic past, it would be the time wasted not understanding how much time needed to go into each assignment. What I did now was at the beginning of every year I looked at my classes, and figured out how much time I needed to spend to make sure that a 3.0 would be possible; because I set my goal to be 3.0. It took some time to get there because I never received a 3.0, so I didn't understand what it would take. Here is one thing that I did understand, I knew for a fact what I was doing would not get to me to the academic goal of a 3.0. So I became married to these goals, I was obsessed with getting a 3.0, my behavior began to change, I started going to the library 4-5 days a week, which I never did in the beginning. I knew that my GPA at this point barely crept above the 2.0 range, and I didn't have a single academic goal in place. So I thought to myself well now that I have these academic goals certainly, I can do better.

What I did was write down on my board when every single assignment was due for the school year. As you can imagine, seeing every single assignment in every class can look overwhelming at first, but it helped me tremendously stay on course for that 3.0. If you are in High school maybe you don't have all your assignments for the semester, ask your teacher (if possible) would they be able to let you know what assignments might be due in the upcoming weeks. Every teacher has to do a lesson plan for the year, so they should have an idea of what assignments are coming up. I would dedicate a certain amount of time for each specific class, I will openly admit Math and I have never gotten along and probably will never get along; so any math classes took hours of time to get prepared for. When you began to set your academic goals, you began to see what classes need the most attention and which ones may need less time.

I am a big advocate of not wasting time, if you are great in a subject, and thoroughly comprehend the material, do yourself a favor and devote a little more time in the subject that might be a little bit more challenging. So every time I felt like I didn't want to study, or I didn't feel like doing an assignment, I would look at the goal I set 3.0. Constantly seeing this 3.0 allowed me to push through those times I didn't feel like doing what was required to receive a 3.0. Am I expecting you to be a perfect student? no I am not, but I am expecting you to be the best student you possibly can be, and one of the tools that will help you accomplish that is academic goal setting. That academic goal needs to become your best friend, you need to treat that academic goal as if it is life or death; yes, it is that serious especially if you are looking to become a better, successful student. I would play a trick on myself that would help me to make sure I would get the 3.0. I would pretend that my college academic advisor told me that if I didn't maintain at least a 3.0 I would be dismissed from the school.

For all my high school students reading this please pretend that your teacher has told you that you wouldn't be able to graduate if you don't maintain the grades you like to have. This kept me on the course to make sure the 3.0 was possible. I would do each assignment before it was actually due, and move on to the next assignment. I remember once in college I had completely finished all my homework assignments in the very first month of the semester for one of my classes! This helped me to free up time to do assignments that were longer, and more time consuming. This also helped me with those subjects I needed to spend a little more time with because they were very challenging. It really comes down to the ultimate goal of what you desire for your academics.

(Exercise)

It is almost impossible to get anything accomplished in life, without goals to look to. So, if we set academic goals, and they don't happen, we have to figure out what was the cause.

Please write down 7 academic goals (it is good to write down goals multiple times) in the first column. In the middle column, put one thing that may stop you from achieving that goal. In the last column, put what can you do to prevent it.

Academic Goal	Obstacle to Achieving Goal	How to Prevent
Raise my grade in English by 1 letter grade.	Spend too much time on social media.	Limit my weekly activity in half on social media

"ACADEMIC GOALS
ONCE
COMPLETED,
BECOME AN
ADDICTION"
-MIKE NELSON

I can't properly put into words as to how addictive conquering your academic goals can become. There truly is power in getting things accomplished, especially those academic goals you set for yourself. Honestly speaking, I never had any true goals before I decided to set academic goals, so for me starting out, seeing results felt good. When I started to see my grades improve, my GPA improve and my assignments coming back with better grades, I knew I could never go back to not having any academic goals. Don't ever think any academic goal is too small, you might have to start off by saying, "This week, in all my classes, I will turn in my work on time."

Don't underestimate the power of starting with those small goals; trust me in the long run, they help to achieve those bigger academic goals. After a while you become accustomed to doing certain things whether (it becomes studying, getting tutoring, etc.) to get the desired academic result. If you look at basketball, those who are champions (Kobe Bryant, Michael Jordan) talk about how winning becomes an addiction. Our attitudes as students must be exactly the same; seeing those goals actually get accomplished will help us want to achieve more academic goals. Which brings me to my next point, because I know you are a highly motivated student (smile). Eventually at some point, the addiction to want to excel more academically will no longer be a want, but a NEED. You will get to a point like I did, and say, "wait a minute, surely I can do more." Please don't be discouraged, yes, you can do it! It will take some time to get adjusted to this new mentality, especially if you have never thought of goal setting when it comes to academics.

Suppose you set your academic goal to end the semester/marking period with a 2.5 and you receive a 2.8. What it means is that next semester, you should now shoot for a minimum of a 3.0. Now some of you might be saying that is too low, and if that is you, great. I will be expecting a 3.5 from you then (smile). But for those of us who may struggle academically, start with something small and work your way up. Here is a thought to consider: you can't become addicted to something that you've never tried. For some who have never tried goal setting, I would challenge you wherever you are in the semester, to start NOW! The beautiful thing about goal setting is that you can start no matter if you're in the beginning of the year, middle or towards the end.

(Exercise)

1. What are your academic goals as of right now? If you do not have any, there is no better time than **NOW!**

   a. _____

   b. _____

   c. _____

2. Take your syllabus / class work, and figure out how much time needs to spent to achieve your academic goals.

3. Whatever those academic goals are, tell them to yourself daily.

4. If you do have academic goals, which new ones can you now set?

   a. _____

   b. _____

   c. _____

5. What do you believe the value is in setting academic goals?

   a. _____

   b. _____

   c. _____

6. In what ways will you benefit from academic goal setting?

   a. _____

   b. _____

   c. _____

7. Complete one academic goal this week and write about how it made you feel. Use a separate piece of paper if you need additional room.

_____

_____

_____

_____

Chapter 4: Discipline

"SUCCESSFUL STUDENTS HOLD EACH OTHER ACCOUNTABLE"

-MIKE NELSON

Often times when we hear the word discipline, we think of something that isn't pleasant. What does discipline look like when it comes to student success? I would define it as doing something you don't like to do, when you necessarily don't feel like it. For example, who likes to wake up early in the morning? I would say not too many people, and most certainly not many students. It's easy to do anything when you feel like it. It's easy to do homework when you feel like it, maybe some of you reading this use to be like me, I never felt like doing homework. There used to be a time when homework was painful to do. I use to be upset when teachers would give homework, especially over the weekend in high school. I remember saying to myself, "You expect us to be in school for 8 hours, and then go home and do homework." I thought it was extremely unfair, and thought the teachers didn't have anything better to do.

It wasn't until I heard in an interview, the great future Hall of Fame linebacker for the Ravens do an interview, and talked about the importance of discipline. Ray Lewis said he made certain sacrifices (not eating fried food) working out consistently. Even though I am sure it was times when he didn't feel like working out, he did it anyway. There will be times when you don't feel like it, please don't let your emotions get in the way of what you know you should be doing. You don't become a successful student based off of feelings. I understand at times school can be boring, and I understand at times you just have days when school is the last thing you might want to do. However, student success is not about what you **FEEL** like. I use to never like to read, but I understood that I needed too. I truly believe that discipline is one of the main reasons that keep students from becoming successful. Especially if you don't like school.

So I started to look at school in a little bit of a different light. One of the main things that made Ray Lewis become successful in college, and later in the NFL, was because he was **DISCIPLINED**. Let us take a look at Ray Lewis. He wasn't a number one recruit coming out of high school. He was considered undersized for his position at linebacker. When he got to the University of Miami in the 90's and started playing, he did such a good job, he was selected number 21 by the Baltimore Ravens, in 1996. Twenty different teams had passed on Lewis because he lacked elite athletic ability. Almost a 20-year career with the Ravens, a two time Super Bowl Champion, and a number of accolades-those teams who passed on Lewis are probably still upset. What those teams didn't understand, which many students don't either, is you don't have to be the smartest to excel, but you must have discipline. From his workouts to the way he played the game, everything was built around discipline.

Ask yourself as a student, "am I disciplined?" There are many of you who want to get certificates, diplomas, and degrees, but are you disciplined enough to receive those things?

It wasn't until I saw a direct connection between my student success and discipline that homework became easier and taking tests became easier. In my Graduate program, I have a professor who says, "discipline, if you stick with it, will eventually turn into delight." That is one of the truest statements I have ever heard. Now you think about it. A good buddy of mine who is a personal trainer told me that if you've never worked out before and start, it will be very difficult in the beginning, but if you stick with it, eventually you will enjoy "the burn" and what you put your body through to achieve the goals you set.

When it comes to academic success, the same rules apply. If you stick with being consistent, and disciplined by doing those assignments and studying, it creates an enjoyable pattern. You start to look forward to doing those assignments and turning them in. Essentially, you look forward to studying (which we will address in a later chapter).

"DON'T LET
**YOUR FEELINGS
GET IN THE WAY**
OF WHAT
{ YOU KNOW }
YOU SHOULD
BE DOING"
-MIKE NELSON

(Exercise)

Discipline is the engine that drives success, if you can get a hold on discipline, you can begin to see a change in your academics. For me as described, math and myself don't have a good relationship. I never liked math, and the thought of it use to make me sick. It wasn't until I understood that math wasn't going anywhere, and for what I was trying to get accomplished academically, I would have to face math head on; without discipline that would be an impossible task.

Often times speaking with students, it's hard for a student to be disciplined in a subject that he or she isn't strong in or doesn't particularly like. Please write down 7 areas academically you aren't disciplined in and write one way for each on how to overcome being undisciplined.

Not Disciplined	How to Overcome

"IF YOU ARE

DISCIPLINED IT'S EASIER

TO STAY FOCUSED"

-MIKE NELSON

The point cannot be stressed enough about the importance of discipline. What is interesting that I discovered was that discipline goes hand in hand with focus. It is almost impossible to be undisciplined, and focused at the same time; just as it is almost impossible to be unfocused and disciplined. You will need both to sustain your academic success. I learned this lesson while I was in college, as I always wondered as to why my grades in the beginning would only improve so much. It was as if I could stop getting D'S and C'S, and get B'S, but it was hard to get into the A range. I had a tough conversation with someone (again going back to having an accountability partner) who I asked to watch my habits for a week, and monitor my progress.

By the time the week was up, I had found out my results; sad but true, I wasn't disciplined enough nor focused enough to reach that new academic level of getting A's that I desired. What I was told was that I was doing a great job being a C and B student, but I didn't do what A students do. So while it was a milestone that I wasn't where I use to be, I had a lot more work and development to get to the next level academically. As you can imagine, this brought on a brand new set of challenges that I didn't anticipate. I had discovered there were certain things "A" students did- and there were certain things I wasn't doing (not yet at least). I questioned whether I would ever be able to become an A student. After all, it was difficult to graduate from the D-C student to a now B student. I questioned how much more it required, what more would need to be done, and was I really able to step up to the challenge?

"**YOU CAN'T**

DESIRE TO BE AN

"A" STUDENT BUT NOT

{ **WANT TO DO** }

WHAT "A" STUDENTS DO"

—MIKE NELSON

I knew that I wanted to grow academically, I just didn't know how or even where to get started. Has that ever been you? You as a student want to do better academically, however you may not have the slightest clue where to begin. If someone could tell you where to begin; to improve that would help.

In speaking and mentoring students, I discovered that **DISCIPLINE** is the #1 thing, even more than not understanding, tests, homework, and different assignments that really can hinder a student from improving. There are far too many students who are not focused and are undisciplined. You can fail a class because you can't handle the tests or assignments, but students also fail for a lack of **DISCIPLINE**. Trust me when I tell you that discipline is not easy, it will take a lifetime to master, as I am writing this I am still trying to focus on being disciplined and master it. I realized that those who were "A" students were disciplined, I realized I could only go so far doing what I was doing. There is an old saying that goes, "the definition of insanity is doing the same thing over and over again and expecting a different result." You do have to make certain choices as a disciplined student, for example, do I want to study, or do I need to go outside and chill with friends?

For you to be disciplined you don't have to use much of your brain. Discipline is not about **HOW YOU FEEL,**

IT'S ABOUT WHAT YOU DO! Unless school is what you love (which there is nothing wrong with that). You probably won't like (studying) every single day which we will address later. So what you have to do is convince yourself that (studying or whatever you don't feel like doing) is actually good for you in the long run. Think about it, you can go outside to "chill" with your friends, or spend time studying to pass a test, that might get you the grade, which may attribute to a high enough GPA to earn a scholarship. Which one seems of more importance? (You can answer that). Am I saying, as a student you should never be allowed to hang with friends or have any social life? Certainly not. But what I am saying is discipline, especially in the beginning, is never fun. Do you know why students don't like discipline? Because it looks as if it has no immediate reward to it. For example, you have to study so many hours a week in order to retain information just to pass a test. You don't get to see the results until after the test, when you may have had to study for the past two weeks. However, if you go and "chill" with your friends, you can go to the mall, get something to eat, go to a party, play sports, put a picture on Instagram, etc.. All of these bring instant satisfaction, while **DISCIPLINE** can be a long, painful process.

(Exercise)

I want you to think about in what ways you are undisciplined. Under **SUBJECT**, write down in what areas/subjects you are not focused in on academically. The middle and last columns, I want you to write a strategy for each on what you will do to help keep you disciplined.

Subject	Strategy #1	Strategy #2
Math	Seek Tutoring	Study More

Chapter 5: Studying

"IF YOU DON'T
STUDY,
YOU HAVE NO RIGHT
TO COMPLAIN ABOUT
THE GRADES YOU GET"
-MIKE NELSON

The game changer for me was studying. I have spoken to hundreds of students, regardless of race, ethnicity, or socioeconomic status, I was shocked to see how little students study, or not study at all. I was also shocked as to how many students didn't even know how to study. From elementary school up until my first year of college, I can't recall a time where studying was ever on the to do list; I just never saw it as important. So when my teachers would ask me if I had studied, I would say sure I did, knowing my textbooks were collecting dust. I remember the first time I attempted to study, saying it was strange probably is an understatement. I picked up my textbook and read for about 5 minutes, and said to myself "studying is boring, and I see why I never studied in the first place." What I was really saying is, that I didn't know HOW to study, and this is primarily the number one reason why I avoided studying the majority of my years in school.

Trying to study for me was like trying to find a set of keys on the beach at night. My problem was I didn't know where to begin. Maybe that is you, deep down you would like to study but honestly, you just don't know how (which can be embarrassing to admit). I remember calling myself "studying" and 99% of the time, I would end up falling asleep or daydreaming, or my mind would be racing with all types of thoughts except studying. I would be frustrated with myself, and really thought at one point that there is no way that people study, they must have a photographic memory or they simply cheat (laughs). It is crazy to think even with my academic challenges (not being good in math or a good writer) that from elementary school, up until college, I never studied and still was managing to pass classes. I had to literally ask myself, how do you even study? Everyone has a different method in which they study. I can only speak to what has worked for me. Once I figured out that it wasn't enough for me to simply "read" the information, things began to look up. So even though I was still up in the air about studying, I knew what studying was not, simply reading information. I had to be able to retain the information until it was time to take the test.

I remember specifically being in a language course, a Greek class. Trying to study for information that I already understood was a challenge, and now I had to study for language I didn't even know. Did I pass the class? Yes! I passed only with letter grade of a B. I taught myself a valuable lesson about studying. How was I able to pass a class that I was unfamiliar with? I learned a lesson or a way of learning and studying the information I needed to remember for my tests. Once you learn this method, it will be so easy for you to retain any information on any subject. I connected everything that I didn't know to something I did know. (**RE-READ THAT**) What do I mean? For example, in Greek the letter G is called Gamma, but in

Greek the shape of the letter reminds me of some type of pull up bar ($\mathbf{\Gamma}$). So every time I would see Gamma in the Greek, I was reminded that it looks like a pull up bar, and that is how I began to learn and to some degree write the language. Another example is that the letter P in the Greek alphabet is called Pi (π). If you're familiar with math, Pi is a **mathematical** constant, the ratio of a circle's circumference to its diameter, commonly approximated as 3.14π which is the Greek name for the letter P. (sorry for my math jargon). So, every time I would have to write the letter P in Greek, I would think of the symbol in math, π. Once I discovered this trick of relating concepts and key terms to something that reminded me of things that I knew, I never failed a test again. This became such a habit, I went from passing with C's, to some A's and majority B's.

(Exercise)

Please answer the following questions.

1. What is it that makes studying difficult?

_____

_____

_____

_____

2. How much time do you actually spend studying?

_____

_____

_____

_____

3. Do you feel as if you were to study more often your grades would improve? Explain why or why not?

_____

_____

_____

_____

4. Do you know how to study?

_____

_____

5. Is there a structure to the way you study? If so, explain.

_____

_____

_____

6. Do you believe you study too much? If so, explain.

_____

_____

_____

7. What are some benefits of studying?

_____

_____

_____

{ **"EVENTUALLY,** }
LIKE EVERYTHING
ELSE IN LIFE,
NOT STUDYING WILL
EVENTUALLY CATCH UP
TO YOU"
-MIKE NELSON

These words would come to be true as I remember being in a history class in college, and the majority of the grades were based on how well you scored on all the exams. To give yourself a chance to pass, you had better been studying weeks in advance. I tried to not study and see how well I would do (I don't recommend ever doing that). I failed the exam with flying colors. It was then I realized that I could no longer avoid studying. I realized that studying and I were going to be headed for a collision course. Not sure if anyone else in the class felt as if they were in trouble, but I knew for a fact I was, but for once, I was determined to do something about it. I remember telling the professor that the exam covered much in the class, and for me, it was overwhelming trying to study all of it.

The professor told me something so simple, but so deep, that it changed the course of how I would study for the rest of my life. He gave me this example. He said to me, "If you were attempting to eat an entire elephant, you wouldn't eat it all at once, right?"

I said to him, "Of course not."

He continued by saying, "What you would do to eat it is, cut the elephant and eat it piece by piece. It will take time, but eventually if you keep eating, you will have eaten the entire elephant."

I didn't understand why he used an elephant for this example, nor did I ever ask. All I knew was that it felt like a light bulb in my brain went off. I got back to my room and looked over the syllabus, and I knew we had two more exams left; a midterm and a final. From looking at the last test, we covered everything from the beginning to almost half of the book. The professor told us what the midterm and final would cover (as far as chapters). So what I did now was what I like to call **power studying**. Power studying is studying in increments of 15 minutes, then you take a 5-minute break, and continue. I didn't wait until the night before, I studied weeks in advance (I was eating the elephant piece by piece).

"DON'T STUDY RANDOMLY, BE VERY INTENTIONAL ABOUT THE WAY YOU STUDY"

-MIKE NELSON

After I figured out how to study, I had to structure my studying. It is very hard to study properly if you are studying all over the place. For me, it was difficult to try to study 3-4 subjects in one day. So what I did was, I began to break up the days that I would study. When trying to study multiple subjects in one day, I noticed that often times I would confuse the information, and my brain would forget a lot of the information. I knew that I wasn't as smart as others, so I knew that my best friend (studying) would help me. For me, studying with structure became like a cheat code; once I was able to add structure to my studying, it became like breathing to me.

Figure out what works for you as a student when it comes to studying. Every student is different and what works for he or she. I had classmates of mine who could study and listen to music at the same exact time; for me that was scary and unproductive. However, just because it didn't work for me doesn't make it wrong. **DON'T LET ANYONE TELL YOU THE WAY YOU STUDY IS WRONG, ESPECIALLY IF YOU HAVE THE GRADES TO PROVE OTHERWISE** (Read that again!)

I need peace and quiet while studying and doing work; the quieter, the better, but not everyone does it the same. Figure out what days you like studying on. As silly as it sounds, I knew for a fact that **I WOULD NEVER** study on Friday and Saturday, I considered Friday and Saturday off limits because of the work that I had put in all week. Who knows, only weekends might work better for you to study (all though I would suggest you study during the week as well). Factor in what hours do you like to study, the best part about studying is you can study whenever you like. For my students not in college this will be a challenge for you (studying when you like) because you are in school for about 8 hours at least. However, maybe weekend mornings before classes work better for you to study, maybe midday or at night. I know for me I like to be an early riser and study during early morning hours or after dinner time 6:00-8:00 p.m. My brain shuts off academically after about 9:00 p.m. So trying to study and do school work is a challenge if it is after this time frame. While you are trying to figure out what habits and tendencies work for you as a student, you will begin to learn habits and tendencies about yourself as well.

"STOP SAYING WHAT YOU WON'T DO AS A STUDENT, WHEN YOU HAVEN'T DISCOVERED IF IT WORKS FOR YOU OR NOT"
-MIKE NELSON

This thing called studying, literally blew my mind. I could not believe all these years, I had failed to take advantage of studying. Once I mastered the art of studying, it literally became a habit. I vowed to myself that I would never be in a class and not commit myself to studying.

Again with my academic challenges I realized that studying would put me in a position to graduate. Studying at first was terrifying, because like often times in life we are scared of the unknown. Me discovering how effective studying was would be the equivalent of finding out as a kid that the "boogie man" wasn't real. I remember saying to myself several times "I was scared all these years for no reason." I realized I had wasted so much time not studying that it ended up costing me potential scholarships, but more importantly learning in general. I can't begin to tell you all the new information I learned along the way. You can learn as much as you need to in class, but with studying you can learn as much as you want to (read that again). It is not as much as how much information you know, (which isn't bad). But I would say you need to know the right information. For example, while it is good to be gifted in geometry, that won't help if you're taking an English test. When studying a subject ask yourself, "What correct information about this subject do I need."

"YOU CAN LEARN
AS MUCH AS
YOU NEED TO
IN CLASS,
BUT WITH STUDYING
YOU CAN LEARN AS
MUCH AS YOU WANT TO"
—MIKE NELSON

This section is for my students who know how to study and have decent grades and GPA's. Being as though I have been on both ends of not knowing how to study, to finally getting the grades I wanted, I knew that there was still another level I could get to. No matter if you're a 3.0 student, or 4.0 student, **YES**, there is still room to improve! And yes, there is still another level of studying that can be learned.

So after I had mastered studying, I started to be creative and challenge myself in the way I studied. *Disclaimer* (You should only do this after you are extremely comfortable with the way you study and your grades should be a reflection of that). So after about 1-2 semesters going from the D'S to high C's and low B's, were good. But I knew that I wanted to reach 89, B+ minimum in all of my grades. What I was doing was working, but soon I realized it didn't quite take me to the next level of grades I desired. I quickly became frustrated. I knew I had matured because I use to get D's and as long as I passed I was okay with that. I was now getting 80-85's and I was highly upset. I thought back to what my professor told me about studying and the example he used of "eating the entire elephant." I knew I had to eat the elephant pieces, but was there something else I was missing? Yes. I discovered that even those pieces could be broken down into smaller pieces. I did something at the time I thought was crazy. I started to make my own study guides for each class. I knew that the majority of my classes had tests, and what would be covered (sometimes).

However, what I was doing before, was not committing myself to reading entire chapters. Instead, I would skim or read half; the crazy part about it was I excelled with doing that. I knew if I wanted to get to that next level, I would have to read as much as possible covering every single sentence in every chapter. After each chapter from the information I read, I would go over and highlight key sentences, phrases, terminology and important dates. I would do this for each chapter.

Did you ever think there was a reason that your professor or teacher would say read all the **REQUIRED READING**, and tell you to read entire chapters? I discovered the reason why I couldn't jump to the "A" range in my grades at first, was because there was information in each chapter that I could not have possibly known without reading **COMPLETE CHAPTERS**.

I asked someone who got high A's, what they did to receive those grades, and they told me, **READ EVERYTHING**, and if necessary, re-read it. I knew that this would take more time, and would be very tedious. However, I began reading complete chapters and putting together my own study guide to go over the information. The high B's and A's started to come in! This next level of studying helped me to become more efficient and a better test taker. Don't worry if you think you won't remember all the information. Your brain has a great capacity to hold much information, but your brain can't, if you don't fill it with anything.

"YOUR BRAIN HAS A GREAT CAPACITY

{ TO HOLD MUCH }

≡ INFORMATION, ≡

BUT YOUR BRAIN CAN'T IF YOU DON'T FILL IT WITH ANYTHING"

{ -MIKE NELSON }

(Exercise)

Please after you are finished reading this chapter look at what chapters you have to read for class, and do me a favor, **READ THEM IN ITS ENTIRETY**. I was shocked when asking (which I shouldn't have because I would do the same) as to how many students skim through chapters. It does take more time to read, but it will help you get to the next level academically.

With the chapters you must read, make a study guide. Highlight key phrases, terms, definitions, and dates for each chapter and write them down in a test form. For math, simply ask your teacher or professor for practice problems (they should be happy to do this) if not, make up your own and learn the method that you need for certain formulas like algebra.

The difference was, I remembered when there were questions on tests that I would think to myself, "I didn't read that, how could that be on the test?" And then I thought, "I am right, I didn't read that while studying." Now those tricky questions on tests, I would say, "I remember reading that." I started getting those A's I desperately coveted.

Chapter 6: Confidence

"YOU GAIN
CONFIDENCE
WHEN YOU HAVE
DONE A TASK
WELL FOR
A PERIOD OF TIME"
-MIKE NELSON

When I interact with students during my motivational presentations, I like to get a feel for where students' confidence is. Often times I simply ask how confident are you in your abilities as a student on a scale of 1-10, 1 being the lowest, and 10 being the highest. Too many times I get students that are somewhere between a 4 and 7. So if we take 5 being the average and majority of the students I speak with say they are in between 4-7, that means they are below confident or just barely confident in their abilities. **WOW!** Confidence I believe is something in education that gets overlooked. When you are confident in your abilities, it gives you that little extra something. Outside of learning disabilities, I believe the majority of students don't do well academically because they lack confidence.

I speak from personal experience; it is very difficult to do a task, especially academics well, if you are not confident. As I sat in on my first college class, I realized that because of my academic challenges, I was fearful of doing any assignments. I'll never forget I was in a class my freshman year of college, and the professor asked what now would be looked at as a simple question, and I remember that I could not answer it. I felt honestly like I didn't belong, and I ended up dropping the course because I thought the class would be too difficult to be in for an entire semester. I remember walking back to my dorm, unable to describe what I was feeling, however, I knew something was missing.

Looking back on that experience it was the big C word that students overlook, **CONFIDENCE**! I wish wherever you are reading this, I could come join you and tell you how important confidence is. What is confidence? Webster's dictionary defines it simply as, "a feeling or belief that you can do something well or succeed at something." Most students, and people in general, don't truly believe that they can do something well.

If you're reading this and maybe you were like me, I use to sit in the back of class, because I knew that those in the back generally weren't expected to participate much. You see, I was well aware of my weaknesses as a student, so I would try to hide them very well. I became very accustomed with my teachers and professors, and knew that they very rarely, if ever, called on students who were in the back, so being in the back, saved me from answering questions. The students who sat in the middle of the class would get called on to answer questions from time to time. Those in the front, almost always would have answers and would have dialect with the teachers about the coursework. Often I thought, "one day" maybe I can be that type of student. I knew for a fact that I wasn't ready yet, and wondered if and when I would ever be able to make that jump.

The best way to be confident is to practice, **YES IT'S THAT SIMPLE!** I am telling you I went from not having confidence to being somewhat confident. I became fully confident in the method that I was using, which we talked about in the previous chapter, which was **STUDYING**. How can you be confident if you don't engage with the subject matter? It's not the fact that you can't do the work, it's the fact that you aren't **CONFIDENT**. It takes time to build confidence- it does not happen overnight, especially when it comes to doing something you may have never done. You as a student have to figure what areas are you strong in and what areas do you need to grow in. The problem is too often we say we want better grades, but we don't know what to do (methods) to make that happen.

Confidence is a two edge sword, if you believe in something (good or bad) it can work to your advantage and your disadvantage, and that's what really confidence is about, **BELIEVING YOU CAN**! For years I was a C-D student because that's what I believed all I could do, so to do anything above that, I never believed it was possible. As a result, I just watched others get good grades, and often knew that I deserved to get grades that my other peers were receiving. What I didn't realize is, that I just needed to become more familiar with the work, so I could believe I could. You heard me say in a previous chapter, that my textbooks at one point in my academic career would literally collect dust (I wasn't exaggerating or lying). You may lack confidence because you may not be doing enough, to become familiar enough with work, that goes back to our chapter on accountability (smile).

"TOO MANY TIMES

STUDENTS WANT BETTER

GRADES, BUT MANY

TIMES THEY DON'T

KNOW HOW TO GET THEM"

{ –MIKE NELSON }

(Exercise)

PART 1: If you were fully confident in your academic abilities, how different would your grades and life be? Please explain.

_____

_____

_____

_____

_____

_____

_____

_____

I discovered when I became confident, it carried over into other areas in my life.

PART 2: Write down in the first column all the areas and subjects in your life that you need to be more confident in. The second column, write down at least one way you plan to become confident in those areas. (Look at my example on the next page in the first row.)

If you need additional space, please use a separate piece of paper.

NEED TO BE MORE CONFIDENT	BECOME MORE CONFIDENT BY
More confident in my writing	Meet with professor. Visit the writing center

Once I met my professor and received the feedback, I knew what I needed to improve on. I started to write, and slowly following the feedback, I started to write better. Which now gave me the confidence to write papers on harder subject matter and I could write papers that were longer. I went from struggling to write 5 page papers, to being able to do 15 page papers with ease. The confidence allowed me to write this book! There is no way I envisioned writing a book in my younger years, but I have the confidence now.

"IT'S HARD TO BE CONFIDENT IN A SUBJECT YOU'RE A STRANGER TO"

-MIKE NELSON

Another word for confidence can be summed up in one word, practice. Look at the life of professional athletes. Yes, I am a big sports fan, and I like to draw inspiration from athletes. For my basketball fans, I don't think anyone would dispute, today in the NBA, Stephen Curry is the best shooter in the game. Please, if you have never seen him play, simply YouTube Stephen Curry Highlights, you will be amazed. He shoots the ball with such accuracy and is so efficient at shooting the basketball, he often looks as if he is toying with defenders. What people tend to overlook is that Stephen Curry could always shoot the basketball, however, not to this extent. You can see it from when he first entered into the NBA in 2009 until now, his confidence has grown! He even made a significant jump from the 2014-2015 season to the 2015-2016 season. Steff Curry said, "I want to practice to the point where it's uncomfortable how fast I shoot, so in the game things kind of slow down."

One of the main reasons he is so comfortable shooting the basketball and so **CONFIDENT** is because he has been practicing. Ask yourself what more do I need to do to become confident? He is confident because he practices! And when its game time in our case (class, or test taking time) he is ready because of the work he has put in! He doesn't wait until it's too late (game time) to figure out what he needs to do, that has already been addressed in practice. He has created scenarios of what to do when certain things happen in practice so he can be ready when it's game time. That gives him the confidence to be fully prepared for whatever happens within the game.

How confident are you when it comes to game time (in the classroom or test taking)? When it comes to playing in an actual game, Stephen Curry performs because of what he is familiar with in practice, which gives him the results needed to defeat his opponent. Soon, his confidence continues to build because of the constant results from game to game. It is the same for us as students, you keep practicing (familiarize yourself with your class work) and when you have to do assignment and tests, you'll have the confidence to get those grades you want, and you keep getting those grades it will continue to give you the confidence that you'll need.

(Exercise)

Think about something you are naturally good at (sports, cooking, dancing, etc.). You are confident in that because you do it on a consistent basis, and you're probably around it often. It's the same with academics. I want you to purposely find a subject or area that you know you aren't confident in. Find out as much about the subject as possible, and spend as much time with it as possible. Do this for 1 month consistently. After the month is up, write down how your confidence has changed and all the things you learned about yourself and the subject during this time.

_____

_____

_____

_____

_____

_____

_____

_____

_____

_____

_____

I really enjoy hearing the definition of confidence, especially the end part, "you can do something well, or become successful in a thing." Confidence goes back to your mind set, **WHAT DO YOU TRULY BELIEVE?** You are reading the words of someone who had a GPA of 1.9 the first year of college, and went onto Graduate school with almost a 3.5 GPA.

Again, I do not say that to brag at all, I want you to see what's possible for your academics and your life, if you would simply **BELIEVE YOU CAN!** Notice with confidence one of the first things that is required is that you **BELIEVE;** simply believing requires no test taking skills, it doesn't require talent, or ability. I want you to see if you can manage to get your confidence at 10. You will feel as if no matter how long a paper is, you can write it and no matter what the subject matter is, you can write about it. Because your confidence will be at a 10, there won't be any math equation, or test you can't pass.

There are some of you reading this who can pass tests and your confidence is around a 5, and this is without studying. Imagine, what would happen if you buckled down and gave 100%? What could happen if your confidence was at a 10? Again, look at Stephen Curry He went from being someone who was a good shooter, to someone who became a great shooter, he went from being someone who could make 3 pointers, to someone who became more efficient when making a 3 point shot. Stephen Curry is someone who I would argue has to do some degree mastered the art of shooting a basketball. Why? Because he brings it back to him simply being confident in his abilities because of what he has done in practice. He doesn't need the coach to tell him "Hey Stephen shoot 1,000 jump shots a day." He did it himself because he realized the more times the ball would go in the basket, the more he would be confident in his ability.

Sometimes that is all it takes, figuratively speaking "you need to see the ball go in the basket." You need to know that you are doing your class work right, you need to get a passing grade on that exam, assignment or paper. When I became confident, and began passing tests, my confidence could never be shaken. The reason why is because I proved to myself that I could do it! Sometimes you need to prove to yourself that you can do what you set out to do, and that helps build your confidence. You should be ready and excited to take your next exam, do that next assignment, to prove to yourself that you can be that student you've always dreamed of! I want you to do something for me, the next time you are about to do any assignment or take a test, I need you to do it confidently. Stop telling yourself well, if I pass I pass, if I don't I don't. Nope, that is not the language of a successful student. Stop psyching yourself out of the assignments and tests before you actually take them. Stop spending so much time and energy on your academic weaknesses that you forget you have some strengths as well. What helped me be confident as well was recognizing "okay Mike, you may not be as smart as others, but you probably have some strengths that others don't have." Reflecting on these strengths as well, helped my confidence to get boosted.

"DON'T SPEND
SO MUCH TIME
ON YOUR ACADEMIC
WEAKNESSES
THAT YOU FORGET YOUR
STRENGTHS AS
A STUDENT"
-MIKE NELSON

(Exercise)

This goes back to our chapter on accountability, and finding an accountability partner. I recommend you ask someone you can trust and will be honest with you. Your partner needs to be someone who can see areas you are strong and weak in, because sometimes we cannot see what others see. Ask your partner to give you feedback on your strengths as well as your weaknesses. After they give you feedback, I want you to write what they said down, and use that to help you build your confidence. Use the list of what your partner, said as a way to look back and see the positives, because you will get frustrated at times. See my example on the next page.

_____

_____

_____

_____

_____

_____

_____

_____

I have often heard I am a person who has persistence. Knowing that helped me to internalize and say to myself, "Well I don't give up easily, so whatever challenges me in subjects, I have to figure a way to learn the material." So, because it's difficult for me to not quit, I took this and applied it to my life and academics, and it help to shape my **CONFIDENCE**.

Chapter 7: Sacrifice

"WHAT SACRIFICES **ARE YOU** WILLING TO { MAKE TO BECOME } **THE STUDENT YOU'VE** ALWAYS WANTED **TO BE?"**

After I had finally realized and identified what I needed to do to become a more successful student, there still was something missing. I had to ask myself, what was I willing to do to make the sacrifice? You see, it is easy to do assignments and pass exams when it doesn't require much of you, if you've always done just enough to pass, or if you aren't looking to improve academically. However, if you're looking to get to the next level as a student, it will cost you something.

This principle of sacrifice is probably the toughest adjustment that I had to make in order to become a better student. From mediocre to good there will be a sacrifice-from good to great there will be a sacrifice as well. Nothing that is worthwhile in life comes at no cost; you will have to pay! Yes, it will be difficult. Yes, you will be frustrated beyond belief, especially when you are trying to grow in certain areas academically. I find it interesting that most students are afraid to sacrifice, **WHY?** Because, often times where you are as a student, is a comfort zone. You know what to expect, especially if you have been doing things for a long time the same way. I am surprised as to how many students are never challenged; certainly not a knock against any teacher, educator or parent. I am just telling the realities from the students whom I have worked with.

Really ask yourself: What am I willing to do to improve? What adjustments can I make?

"YOU HAVE TO

SACRIFICE

{ TO GET TO }

THE ULTIMATE PRIZE"

{ -MIKE NELSON }

Knowing exactly what you want is the key to your success as a student, how can you sacrifice for something you are unsure of? Again, this goes back to our chapter on setting goals. I have no idea what level you are trying to reach in your academics, but I do know that if you are striving to be a better student, it will come at some cost! The best example I can use is going back and looking at when LeBron James left a comfortable situation in Cleveland to go to a place that was unfamiliar, Miami. Along with Chris Bosh, Dwayne Wade; a team with their top 3 players being All-Stars. Dwayne Wade and Chris Bosh were more impacted specifically. Before LeBron James arrival Bosh and Wade were both the best players on their other teams (Bosh in Toronto and Wade with Miami). When coming together question arose as to who would be the best player, I'll never forget the report that came out and Wade told James that it was his team and he had the green light to be the best player. Dwayne Wade understood that LeBron and himself, could not and would not win a championship (the ultimate goal) with both of them trying to be the best player. He understood that LeBron was better, and he needed to sacrifice his own game to win. Keep in mind that Dwayne Wade was a champion before LeBron arrived in Miami, LeBron was not. By Dwayne Wade sacrificing he and the Miami Heat won back to back NBA championships. The goal was accomplished!

What do you want? Are you looking to pass a test, or are you looking to improve your GPA? Let's be clear, Dwayne Wade didn't sacrifice to win a game, he sacrificed to win a championship. It is not enough to sacrifice without being specific as for your reason for doing it. What is the ultimate goal at the end of the sacrifice? You must, must, must have what I like to call "sacrificial goals," things that you are willing to give up, to see those goals happen. One of mine was to cut back on playing basketball in the gym frequently to put more focus on my studies. So instead of playing 5-6 days a week, I would play 2-3 times a week, and spend the time I wasn't playing to focus on my academics.

(Exercise)

Write down 7 different sacrificial goals that will help you to improve academically?

Sacrificial Goals	

"ON THE
OTHER SIDE
OF THE SACRIFICE
{ IS THE GRADES }
YOU'VE
ALWAYS
DREAMED OF"
-MIKE NELSON

I get it, I promise you, I really do! There are some of you out there who are skeptical. You might be thinking, Mike, "What if I do all this sacrificing" and it still doesn't work? My question back to you is, "What is the alternative?"

What would happen if you don't sacrifice? Stop and think about this for a second. You would most likely keep getting the same results. Since I know you are looking to improve and do better, the only way to do that is to sacrifice. It will not end with you failing if you are willing to put in the work and study. If you are willing to place more time on your academics, it has to happen! Again, I was skeptical myself, but what I discovered was you can't complain about the grades you don't have, from the sacrifices you didn't make. Do you really think that it will end in defeat if you made the necessary sacrifices? The real challenge is to look at your life and figure out what areas do sacrifices need to be made in. Do you need to study longer, change your friends, go to bed earlier, or stop watching TV as much? What is it? For me it was spending so much time on social media. Realizing that social media didn't push me anywhere closer to my ultimate goal of becoming a better student.

On the next exercise you'll see what the power of sacrifice can do, and what you can get accomplished. My cell phone was a big sacrifice that I had to give up, because it seemed like as soon as I was ready to do assignments, texts and phone calls would come in. I knew I was spending too much time on my phone, so much time that I would only be able to get a certain amount of work done, it was frustrating honestly. So I decided to do something crazy. Whenever I had to write a paper, I decided to not put my phone on airplane mode, but to power it off. Yes, I am not telling you that you need to be as drastic as I was-no I take that back, for some of you, yes! Give up that cell phone, TV, and whatever else it takes! I discovered that I was able to be more focused, get more assignments done, and study better.

The crazy part was, when I really think about it, those conversations on the phone and text weren't important and could wait. It hurt to turn my cell phone off, but the more I did it, the easier it became over time. When I started out, I could only go about 15 minutes before I had to power it back on. I slowly increased to 30 minutes, and then an hour.

Now, when I really need to focus, I can go hours without my phone. It wasn't always this way; it takes time to build up to that level. I know that it can get difficult and I know it can sometimes seem impossible, however, you have to ask yourself whatever it is that won't allow me to sacrifice is it really worth it? I would like to say 95% of the time, no!

"YOU CAN'T
COMPLAIN
ABOUT THE GRADES
YOU DON'T GET
FROM THE
SACRIFICES YOU
DON'T MAKE"
{   -MIKE NELSON   }

(Exercise)

This particular exercise will take one week to complete. Please write down as many distractions that are holding you back, from making the necessary sacrifices, from becoming a better student.

Write down how many hours does that take up of your time. Do this for a complete week. After the week, look at how much time was spent doing useless things. So if you spent 6 hours doing useless things replace that with something that will help you to become a better student. (Hint... Studying.)

Distraction	Time of Distraction

Distraction	Time of Distraction

Distraction	Time of Distraction

{ **"THERE IS** }

NO EXCUSE FOR NOT

LIVING UP TO

YOUR FULL

ACADEMIC POTENTIAL"

—MIKE NELSON

We have come to the conclusion of the book, all 7 Keys to Student Success. These are direct principles tried, tested and true, that allowed me to go from being an academic risk student to being a successful master's degree student. What happened? I had to learn the 7 keys to student success through trial and error. I spent many nights wondering if I could ever be the student I desired to be. The answer of course was yes! However, it would take many different tools and resources to help get me there.

You have the keys to student success no matter what academic level you might find yourself on. You have a blueprint that has worked, and has been given to hundreds of students from elementary school to college. The only way you will see a change, is if you believe you can, and I am here to tell you that, **YOU CAN**!

If a kid from West Philly can go from academic risk student, scoring well below average on the SAT'S to college graduate and now to successful master's degree student, why can't you? Again, I don't say that to brag, I say that to let you know what is possible, if you dare to put the 7 keys to the test. There is absolutely no excuse for not living up to your **FULL** academic **POTENTIAL**!

There is no reason why you can't make honor roll-no excuse as to why you can't be a 3.0 and above student- and absolutely no excuse of why you can't get that degree. I believe in you, and so should you! It is time for you to start being the student you've always desired. It is time for you to see what academic success tastes like. It is time for you to get the grades that you **WANT**, not only **NEED**, but want! That is the power of the 7 Keys to Student Success. It will allow you to have confidence in yourself, but also to have confidence in your abilities.

Right now you never have to live another day in academic mediocrity; you deserve to be mentioned in the same sentence with all the rest of the top performers of your peers. The 7 Keys to Student Success will allow you to go from a good student to a great student! I hope this book has taken you to a whole different level-academically and personally.

I HOPE YOU ARE READY TO BECOME THE STUDENT YOU'VE ALWAYS DESIRED TO BE!

I hope you will find this book useful. Your suggestions and feedback are most welcome. Please send an email to: info@mikenelsonspeaks.com.

Thank you! Here is to reaching your greatest academic potential and all the greatness in your life.

Mike Nelson

{ "THE ONLY }

PERSON STOPPING
YOU FROM BECOMING

A SUCCESSFUL STUDENT,

IS THE PERSON

WHO YOU LOOK

AT EVERYDAY IN THE

MIRROR... YOU"

-MIKE NELSON

Resources

XVI According to E. F. Schumacher, "Any intelligent fool can make things bigger, more complex, and more violent. It takes a touch of genius—and a lot of courage to move in the opposite direction." Small is Beautiful, an essay, in The Radical Humanist, Vol. 37, No. 5 (August 1973), p. 22.

6 "You are the total sum of the 5 people you surround yourself with." Jim Rohn, The Art of Success (1991) Source: Holmqvist (1991), p. 69

76 According to Albert Einstein (1951), "doing the same thing over and over again and expecting different results."

102 Merriam-Webster's collegiate dictionary (10th ed.). (1993). Springfield, MA: Merriam-Webster.

Special Thanks /Acknowledgements

I want to thank my Father for being the support system that I could always depend on.

I would like to thank my cousin Greg, who has always encouraged me to never settle, and to dream big.

Thanks to my best friend Caster who from day one always believed in me

I would like to thank my friend who is more like a brother, Tim, thanks for your inspiration and encouragement.

I want to thank my good friends from the Wolfpack, and Starting 5, you guys have been more instrumental than you'll ever know.

To my favorite teacher Mr. Sapp thank you for simply believing in me.

To all my professors and teachers throughout the years, thank you for teaching me not only academics but life lessons.

Thanks to my higher power, and when I refer to higher power I am talking about my Lord Jesus Christ.

Finally, to everyone who has ever supported me and my efforts to attempt to change the trajectory of students' lives thank you as well.

65078537R00087

Made in the USA
Charleston, SC
09 December 2016